DEFINING EVENTS
of the Twenty-First Century

# WAR AND TERRORISM

in the Twenty-First Century

by Blythe Lawrence

ReferencePoint Press®

San Diego, CA

For more information, contact:
ReferencePoint Press, Inc.
PO Box 27779
San Diego, CA 92198
www.ReferencePointPress.com

LIBRARY OF CONGRESS CATALOGING-IN-PUBLICATION DATA

Names: Lawrence, Blythe, author.
Title: War and terrorism in the twenty-first century / Blythe Lawrence.
Description: San Diego, CA : ReferencePoint Press, [2020] | Series: Defining
  events of the twenty-first century | Audience: Grade 9 to 12. | Includes
  bibliographical references and index.
Identifiers: LCCN 2019005378 (print) | LCCN 2019019532 (eBook) | ISBN
  9781682826102 (eBook) | ISBN 9781682826096 (hardcover)
Subjects: LCSH: Terrorism--Juvenile literature. | War--Juvenile literature. |
  Terrorism--Prevention--Juvenile literature. | Conflict
  management--Juvenile literature.
Classification: LCC HV6431 (ebook) | LCC HV6431 .L397 2020 (print) | DDC
  303.6/6--dc23
LC record available at https://lccn.loc.gov/2019005378

# CONTENTS

# IMPORTANT EVENTS

## 2006
Saddam Hussein is executed after being found guilty of crimes against humanity.

## 2007
More US soldiers die in Iraq than in any year since the Iraq War began in 2003.

## 2003
The United States invades Iraq in March, intending to crush the regime of President Saddam Hussein.

## 2008
The Taliban in Afghanistan shows its resilience, surprising US troops at the Battle of Wanat.

2000    2002    2004    2006    2008

## 2001
Nearly 3,000 people die in the September 11 terrorist attacks that topple the World Trade Center buildings in New York and damage the Pentagon. In response, the United States sends troops to Afghanistan to root out terrorist groups there.

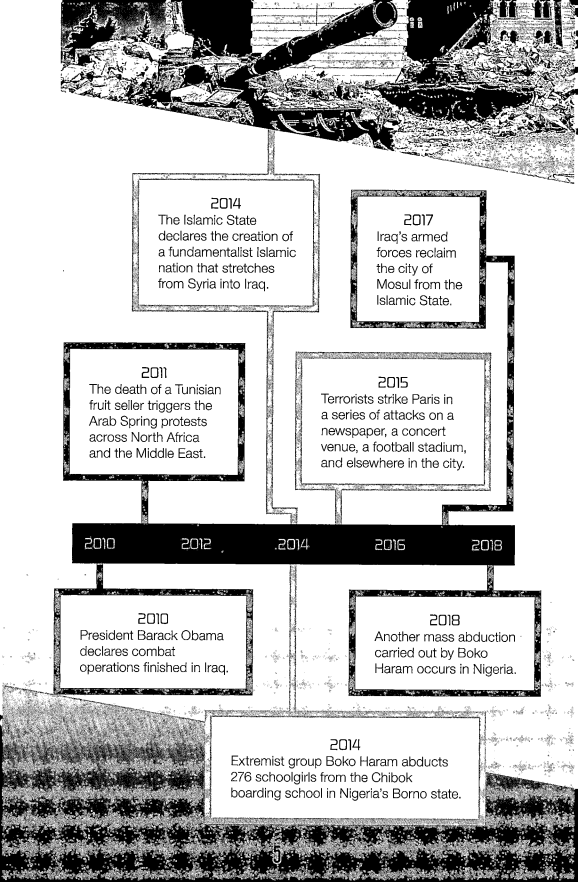

**2014**
The Islamic State declares the creation of a fundamentalist Islamic nation that stretches from Syria into Iraq.

**2017**
Iraq's armed forces reclaim the city of Mosul from the Islamic State.

**2011**
The death of a Tunisian fruit seller triggers the Arab Spring protests across North Africa and the Middle East.

**2015**
Terrorists strike Paris in a series of attacks on a newspaper, a concert venue, a football stadium, and elsewhere in the city.

2010    2012    2014    2016    2018

**2010**
President Barack Obama declares combat operations finished in Iraq.

**2018**
Another mass abduction carried out by Boko Haram occurs in Nigeria.

**2014**
Extremist group Boko Haram abducts 276 schoolgirls from the Chibok boarding school in Nigeria's Borno state.

# An American Nightmare

**M**uch of America was still asleep at 8:46 a.m. on the morning of September 11, 2001, when the street sounds of New York City were swallowed by the heavy roar of a jet airliner flying at close range overhead. Several blocks from the World Trade Center, a complex of buildings centered on twin 110-story towers, filmmaker Jules Naudet instinctively turned his camera toward the sound. Naudet and his brother had been making a documentary about New York Fire Department firefighters. That morning, the firefighters were responding to a gas leak that had been reported near the World Trade Center.

Naudet and the firefighters were at the location of the leak when they heard the aircraft above them. They watched in horror as the jet slammed into the upper floors of the north tower of the World Trade Center, leaving a smoking black hole in the facade of the building. It was the opening act of a nightmare. Seventeen minutes later, at 9:03 a.m., a second plane flew into the south tower, exploding into a massive fireball. It became clear that the first plane crash had been no accident. Terrorists had hijacked airliners and were flying them on suicide missions into their targets. About an hour after the second

After the airliners hit the towers, huge clouds of black smoke billowed from the upper floors. The raging fires weakened the structures, leading to their collapse.

plane hit, Naudet was filming the firefighters in the lobby of the North Tower when he heard an ominous rumble.

The firefighters understood what was happening first. "I saw something I'd never, never seen in a firefighter's eyes: uncertainty, disbelief," Naudet recalled. "Then I remember hearing a rumble, and everyone starts to run like crazy. The roar is getting louder and louder as I run. The light changes and everything becomes pitch black. I definitely think the building is coming down. I was afraid of dying. . . .

I stop, crouch down, just waiting for the ceiling to crash on me. There is a strange calm."[1]

By this time, millions of Americans were glued to their television screens and watching the events unfold live. At 9:59 a.m., fifty-six minutes after being struck by United Airlines Flight 175, the south tower of the World Trade Center collapsed to the ground. Less than an hour later, the north tower, hit by American Airlines Flight 11, also plummeted to the earth. The collapse of both enormous skyscrapers sent steel, glass, and bodies crashing hundreds of feet to the ground as people ran away in all directions. "This," commented one eyewitness, "is what hell looks like, in case you'd ever stopped to wonder."[2]

> **"This is what hell looks like, in case you'd ever stopped to wonder."[2]**
>
> —An eyewitness to the terrorist attacks of September 11, 2001, in New York City

## Aftermath

In a matter of seconds, the bright morning was transformed into an apocalyptic scene of gray rubble, smoke, and debris. A mammoth cloud of dust choked the air. Thousands of people charged through the streets of New York, fleeing for their lives in a mass evacuation of Lower Manhattan. Fearing further attacks from an unknown foe, a number of other landmarks around the country, including the Sears Tower in Chicago, Illinois, were evacuated. For the first time ever, US airspace was closed. All flights already in progress over or bound for the United States were ordered to land.

That morning, President George W. Bush was in Florida, visiting an elementary school. From the school, the president acknowledged the event, calling it "an apparent terrorist attack on our country."

"Today, we've had a national tragedy," he said. "I have spoken to the Vice President, to the Governor of New York, to the Director of the FBI, and have ordered that the full resources of the federal government go to help the victims and their families, and to conduct a full-scale investigation to hunt down and to find those folks who committed this act. Terrorism against our nation will not stand."[3]

New York City mayor Rudy Giuliani was on the street near the towers. The area where the attacks occurred would become known as Ground Zero. Giuliani described September 11 as "one of the most difficult days in the history of the city and the country. The tragedy that we're all undergoing right now is something that we've had nightmares about but probably thought wouldn't happen. . . . The number of casualties will be more than any of us can bear, ultimately."[4]

As the horror unfolded in New York, it became clear that the Twin Towers had not been the attackers' only target. Two more planes bound for California had also been hijacked in midair and redirected eastward. American Airlines Flight 77 made it to Washington, DC, where it hit the western side of the Pentagon, the headquarters of the United States Department of Defense. One hundred and eighty-nine people, including the sixty-four on board, were killed. On the other airliner, United Airlines Flight 93, passengers revolted against the hijackers, ultimately leading the plane to crash into a field in Pennsylvania before the attackers could reach another target. There were no survivors.

In the first few confusing hours, no one knew where the attackers had come from, what they wanted, or why they had done what they did. In all, nearly 3,000 people died in the attacks. They weren't the only victims. Thousands more were wounded as they fled lower Manhattan. Additionally, many of those who helped clean up the debris at Ground Zero in the days, weeks, and months after

The towers' collapse coated the surrounding area with debris and dust. The toxic smoke caused illness in many of the rescue and cleanup workers.

September 11 later contracted respiratory illnesses that eventually claimed their lives.

The political and economic reverberations of September 11, 2001, were not just felt in the United States. The attacks ushered in an era of fear and uncertainty and made *terrorism* a household word. They led US troops to engage in long-term conflicts in the Middle East that continued to evolve over the subsequent decades. One of those conflicts, the War in Afghanistan, continued into 2019, lasting longer than any other war in US history.

Speaking several days after the attacks, President Bush summed up the new attitude of the American government:

*Tonight we are a country awakened to danger and called to defend freedom. Our grief has turned to anger, and anger to resolution. Whether we bring our enemies to justice, or bring justice to our enemies, justice will be done. . . . All of this was brought upon us in a single day—and night fell on a different world, a world where freedom itself is under attack.[5]*

With the events of a single morning, the US perspective on world affairs shifted dramatically. America would become more proactive in rooting out terrorism and acting to curtail it—using force if necessary—in an effort to protect its citizens from another attack like the ones on September 11, 2001.

In the twenty-first century, technological advancements have equipped conflicting parties with weapons ranging widely in sophistication, from high-tech drones and laser-targeted missiles to improvised roadside bombs and rusty, decades-old machine guns. Unlike wars of previous centuries, where military victory often hinged on cavalry charges and grand flanking maneuvers, the conflicts of the 2000s and 2010s have often been exhausting campaigns against shadowy enemies who plant bombs or wreak havoc during suicide missions. Some experts have considered these to be unwinnable wars, while others have declared them essential to national security. Such conflicts have stretched from weeks to months to years without anyone emerging as a clear winner.

# Chapter 1

# What Happened in Afghanistan and the War on Terror?

In the days following September 11, 2001, Americans racked their brains trying to understand what would cause nineteen men to hijack four airplanes and cause the deaths of nearly 3,000 people. The biggest question was why. Why was the United States being targeted, and what had driven terrorists to murder thousands of innocent people?

## The Making of a Militant

The US government's suspicion quickly centered around al Qaeda, a militant organization founded by Osama bin Laden during the 1980s. The son of a Saudi Arabian construction billionaire, Bin Laden had grown up in the lap of luxury in Saudi Arabia. While attending university, he was exposed to new ideas about Islam. His new mentors taught Bin Laden that the life of pleasure he and his family led was deeply sinful. In their opinion, the true path of Islam was jihad, an Arabic word meaning "holy struggle." Their interpretation of *struggle* meant *violence*—violence against anyone who did not share their particular beliefs. The goal, which Bin Laden eagerly adopted, was to

Osama bin Laden agreed to a handful of interviews in the 1990s to explain his ideology. Over the course of decades, his terrorist group was responsible for thousands of murders.

eradicate all Western influence from the Middle East and to reshape the region into a purely Islamic state.

In 1998, Bin Laden incited his followers to kill Americans everywhere. Murdering an American was an "individual duty" for all Muslims, he claimed.[6] In an interview with *Time* magazine the next year, he declared: "I am confident that Muslims will be able to end the legend of the so-called superpower that is America."[7]

## The Gathering Storm

For all that, many Americans at the turn of the century still didn't know who Osama bin Laden was. The American government was watching and learning, however. By the spring of 2001, the Central Intelligence

> **"The world felt like it was on the edge of an eruption."[8]**
>
> — CIA director George Tenet on the months before September 11, 2001

Agency (CIA) had drawn a startling conclusion: the United States would very possibly be the victim of a terrorist attack. "The world felt like it was on the edge of an eruption," said George Tenet, the director of the CIA from 1997 to 2004.[8] In a meeting that July, Secretary of State Condoleezza Rice was warned that al Qaeda would likely attack the United States within the next few months, though nobody had any information about exactly where or when it would take place. The attack came on September 11.

The term *war* was first mentioned by President Bush in a speech several days after the attack. "We're at war. There's been an act of war declared upon America by terrorists, and we will respond accordingly," Bush proclaimed.[9] In the following days, the US government authorized the use of military force against those responsible for the 9/11 attacks. Bush pledged to defeat terrorist organizations, beginning with al Qaeda and ending with state-sponsored terrorism, which is when governments know about terrorist organizations within their countries and help them in some way. The United States had identified those who had planned the September 11 attacks. The new question was, how would the country respond?

## A New Kind of Conflict

The US government believed Bin Laden and al Qaeda were hiding in Afghanistan, sheltered by the Taliban government. On September 20, nine days after the attacks, President Bush accused al Qaeda of planning and carrying out the attacks. Though none of the nineteen hijackers were citizens of Afghanistan, al Qaeda was based in that country. Therefore, Bush argued, the government of Afghanistan was partly responsible for what had happened.

"We will make no distinction between the terrorists who committed these acts and those who harbor them," Bush said.[10] Several days later, he delivered an ultimatum to Afghanistan. "Americans are asking: Who attacked our country? The evidence we have gathered all points to a collection of loosely affiliated terrorist organizations known as al-Qaeda," he said. "Al-Qaeda is to terror what the mafia is to crime. But its goal is not making money, its goal is remaking the world—and imposing its radical beliefs on people everywhere."[11]

Bush demanded that the Taliban turn over al Qaeda's leaders to the United States and that the terrorist organization's training camps be closed. "These demands are not open to negotiation or discussion," Bush added.[12] The implication was clear: if Afghanistan did not comply with the demands, the United States would use force.

What Bush outlined on September 20 was a new kind of war. Even then, he seemed to have a sense that this war would be a long one. Unlike most previous conflicts, which featured large opposing forces and decisive battles, the hunt for terrorists would be on a smaller scale. Rooting out terrorists would take time. "This war will not be like the war in Iraq a decade ago, with a decisive liberation of territory and a swift conclusion," he warned. "Americans should not expect one battle, but a lengthy campaign, unlike any other we have ever seen."[13]

# Operation Enduring Freedom

The Taliban refused to turn Bin Laden over to the Americans, so as September drew to a close, American armed forces prepared to invade Afghanistan. Their mission became known as Operation Enduring Freedom.

In early October, the United States, with the help of the United Kingdom, began bombing Afghanistan from the air, aiming to destroy al Qaeda's training camps and sites important to the Taliban government. The airstrikes focused on three cities: Kabul, Kandahar, and Jalalabad. US ground troops entered the country. As the days passed, the Tora Bora Mountains in eastern Afghanistan, near the border with Pakistan, became a focus of the combat. US leaders believed al Qaeda's forces had fallen back into the mountains and hid in a network of caves.

On November 13, forces of the Northern Alliance, a political faction that had opposed the Taliban, captured the capital city of Kabul. The troops continued to gain ground on the Taliban. Bin Laden fled east across the border and took refuge in Pakistan. He would elude capture for several years.

The city of Kandahar and the strategic border town of Spin Boldak were the last holdouts of the Taliban. Finally, on December 7, 2001, they, too, surrendered. For the moment, the Taliban had been driven from central Afghanistan and into the white-capped mountains of Spin Ghar. The search for Bin Laden continued.

# New Beginnings and Backslides

American military operations in Afghanistan in the fall and winter of 2001 weakened the influence of the Taliban and al Qaeda, but they

did not eliminate these groups entirely. At the Bonn Conference
hosted by the United Nations in Germany in November 2001, the first
steps toward forming a new government for Afghanistan were taken.
Hamid Karzai was chosen as the country's interim leader. In 2004,
Karzai became the country's first democratically elected president.

The International Security Assistance Force (ISAF), led by the
United States, was also established at this meeting. The purpose of

## A Voice for Change

Not all Arabs subscribe to Bin Laden's brand of Islam. Like Bin Laden,
Ahmad Shah Massoud fought against the Soviet troops in Afghanistan
during the 1980s. But Massoud had a different conception of both his
faith and his country's future. He later became a military commander
against the Taliban regime. Massoud, known as "The Lion of Panjshir,"
was a cultured man who loved poetry and supported women's rights.

Massoud brought together ethnic leaders from different areas
in Afghanistan. Their 1996 agreement to work together became the
Northern Alliance, the homegrown challenger to the Taliban. In a press
conference in early 2001, Massoud begged for aid for the Afghan people.
"If I could say one thing to President [George W.] Bush, it would be that if
he doesn't take care of what is happening in Afghanistan the problem will
hurt not only the Afghan people but the American people as well," he said.

Aided by US troops, the Northern Alliance eventually drove the
Taliban out of power. However, Massoud did not live to see it. Two
days before the September 11 attacks, a pair of assassins posing as
journalists were granted an interview with Massoud. They detonated a
bomb concealed in a television camera. Massoud died before reaching
a hospital. September 9, the day of his death, is now a national holiday
in Afghanistan.

*Quoted in Sebastian Junger, "Massoud's Last Conquest," Vanity Fair, February 2002.*
*www.vanityfair.com.*

the force was to train Afghan troops and guard citizens against the Taliban forces still in Afghanistan. The United Kingdom, Canada, and many nations from western Europe contributed soldiers to the effort. Leaders were cautiously hopeful that a new day had dawned for the nation. "We're holding our breath," one diplomat said.[14]

Despite the efforts of the ISAF forces, the Taliban proved a hard rival to defeat once and for all. New Taliban fighters flowed continuously into Afghanistan from Pakistan's border regions, where Taliban rule had also taken hold. The insurgents relied mainly on hit-and-run tactics, opening fire and then retreating into the caves or bunkers in the mountains. As a result, no matter how many troops the United States poured into Afghanistan, the country remained extremely hard to control.

The use of improvised explosive devices (IEDs) also entered into play. Taliban fighters took to hurling IEDs into ISAF military convoys or planting bombs on the roadside, killing or maiming the soldiers in the vehicles. These surprise attacks, which often took place one after the other, happened when soldiers were patrolling an area or driving convoys from one place to the next. They were responsible for large numbers of ISAF casualties and also provided a layer of uncertainty that kept soldiers on edge at all times.

In the hours before dawn on July 13, 2008, almost 200 Taliban fighters attacked a new outpost set up by American and Afghan forces at Wanat, in the remote hilly terrain near the Afghanistan-Pakistan border. The coordination and sophistication of the attack took the US military by surprise. The insurgents were able to penetrate the base, something that would not have happened if the Americans had been adequately prepared.

Wanat resulted in nine US deaths, the most of any attack since 2005. Taliban leaders celebrated the victory. "The fighting in

British troops patrolled the city of Kandahar after driving Taliban forces out. Troops from many nations have taken part in the War in Afghanistan.

Afghanistan is getting heavier. When the Americans drop bombs on civilians, ordinary people want revenge—that's why they are joining the Taliban, strengthening us," a Taliban spokesman said. "Now, instead of firing at the bases from far away, the Taliban has the ability to enter the bases and kill Americans."[15] ISAF responded by withdrawing from Wanat. To critics, the attack justified complaints that the United States did not have an adequate number of troops in the country.

Another significant clash, the Battle of Kamdesh, came in October 2009. Approximately 300 Taliban troops attacked Combat Outpost

Keating in eastern Afghanistan, just 20 miles (32 km) from Wanat. Though the Taliban lost half its force, eight Americans were killed in the battle and another twenty-seven were wounded. A report issued by the US military after the event brought into question why Keating had even existed in the first place. The outpost had "no tactical or strategic value," according to the report, and had been attacked nearly fifty times already that year.[16] Intelligence reports had warned that another attack was likely, but the intelligence had been ignored. Even so, when the outpost was attacked, aid was slow to arrive.

# Protests and Increased Troop Numbers

The United States tried to gain the upper hand by increasing the number of troops in Afghanistan. In 2009, new US president Barack Obama made the decision to send an additional 30,000 troops to Afghanistan, a surge of fresh manpower that brought the US commitment there to nearly 100,000 soldiers. "This increase is necessary to stabilize a deteriorating situation in Afghanistan, which has not received the strategic attention, direction and resources it urgently requires," Obama said. "The Taliban is resurgent in Afghanistan, and al-Qaeda supports the insurgency and threatens America from its safe haven along the Pakistani border."[17]

In early 2011, Obama was informed that US intelligence officials believed they knew where Bin Laden was hiding: a compound in Abbottabad, Pakistan. A team of US Navy special forces troops flew into the country secretly in the middle of the night using two modified Black Hawk helicopters. The elite troops arrived at the compound, located Bin Laden, and killed him. Obama announced the successful mission in a television address shortly afterward.

By this time, there were nearly 140,000 total ISAF troops in Afghanistan. Ten years after the 9/11 attacks, the United States was still trying to hold the Taliban at bay and maintain order in the embattled country. By many indications, it was not going well.

Obama decided he had seen enough. In June 2011, he announced that 33,000 soldiers would return home to the United States by the end of 2012. Against the advice of critics, including some military commanders, Obama also said that US combat operations would cease in the region by the end of 2014, allowing the ISAF-trained Afghan forces to take over.

"We have put al-Qaeda on a path to defeat," the president declared, calling it "a victory for all who have served since 9/11."[18] But the events of the following months called the statement into question. As the ten-year anniversary of September 11, 2001, approached, the

## The Death of Bin Laden

Two Black Hawk helicopters lifted off from Jalalabad, Afghanistan, crossed the border into Pakistan, and headed for a small community near the mountains 120 miles (190 km) from their departure point. The twenty-three US Navy SEALs on board had been charged with a special mission: infiltrate the three-story white compound where Osama bin Laden was suspected to be hiding and capture or kill the elusive al-Qaeda leader once and for all.

On May 2, 2011, the SEALs slipped into Pakistan and cautiously entered the house. After a brief battle in which several people were killed, Bin Laden was isolated and shot. The SEALs verified his identity and took the body with them. In accordance with Muslim traditions, he was buried at sea. The raid on the Abbottabad compound brought an intense ten-year manhunt to an end. But it did not deter the organization Bin Laden helped found. Al-Qaeda carried on without him.

The death of Bin Laden was a major news story. Nearly a decade after the September 11 attacks, their architect had finally been found and killed.

Taliban stepped up its attacks. On September 10, a suicide bomber set off a truck bomb at the entrance of an ISAF base in Wardak in eastern Afghanistan. The blast injured dozens of American troops.

## Freedom's Sentinel and Resolute Support

On December 28, 2014, ISAF's activities in Afghanistan drew to a close as responsibility for the security of the country was formally transferred to Afghan forces. The same year, the United States and

Afghanistan signed a security agreement permitting the United States to maintain a military presence in Afghanistan through 2024 in a new operation called Operation Freedom's Sentinel, which is aimed at training and advising the Afghan military. Likewise, the North Atlantic Treaty Alliance (NATO), a military alliance between European and North American countries, has kept a smaller number of forces in Afghanistan on a mission named Resolute Support. Even while ending some combat missions, NATO and the US government claimed that victory in Afghanistan was theirs. "Thanks to the remarkable effort of our forces, we have achieved what we set out to do," read a NATO communication. "Together, we have created the conditions for a better future for millions of Afghan men, women and children."[19]

Between 2001 and 2019, more than 2,200 Americans died in the conflict in Afghanistan. The number of civilian deaths in Afghanistan is much higher. Experts estimate it has topped 30,000. Additionally, the war is estimated to have cost the United States $840 billion.

Still, the fighting goes on. In the year 2016, an average of twenty-two Afghan troops lost their lives every day. Some of the Afghan forces trained by ISAF and the United States have disappeared with weapons paid for by the US government. In July 2018, US Army soldier Joseph Maciel was killed by a member of the security forces he was sent to Afghanistan to train. Taliban presence in Afghanistan has not been eradicated. Rather, in 2018, the Taliban was said to control or contest 50 to 60 percent of Afghanistan's districts.

By 2019, nearly two decades after the September 11 attacks, there was no end in sight. "The continuation of the conflict, now nearly a generation long, also means that people who can't even remember the attacks are old enough to deploy," a journalist from the *Atlantic* noted in 2018. "Soon people who weren't even born then will be old enough to go fight."[20]

# Chapter 2

# What Happened in the Iraq War?

O n September 12, 2002, almost exactly one year after the 9/11 attacks, the news that American military personnel under the command of General Tommy Franks were on the move appeared in the *New York Times*. "By moving much of General Franks's headquarters staff to the gulf, the United States will take an important step toward mounting a military campaign in Iraq," the *Times* reported. "In essence, the American military is trying to put things in place so it has a running start in any campaign."[21]

Iraq was indeed the focus of the Bush administration. With Operation Enduring Freedom and the hunt for Osama bin Laden underway in Afghanistan, the US government was turning its attention to a different person, one it said posed a serious threat to the security of the United States: Iraqi president Saddam Hussein.

## Old Shadows, New Concerns

The United States and Saddam Hussein's Iraq had long been foes. In August 1990, Iraq invaded Kuwait, its much smaller neighbor to the south. Iraqi soldiers quickly overran the country, and Saddam Hussein

Saddam Hussein was a dictator who ruled through violence and oppression. He controlled Iraq for more than two decades.

announced that Kuwait had become a province of Iraq. Iraq said it had a right to claim Kuwait because both countries had once been part of the Ottoman Empire. Many suspected the Ottoman connection was just an excuse. Thanks to its vast oil fields, Kuwait was a rich nation. Iraq, however, was deeply in debt due to an eight-year war with Iran that had recently ended.

The United Nations and even many of Iraq's allies condemned the invasion. The United Nations gave Iraq an ultimatum: withdraw from Kuwait within forty-five days or face the consequences. When Saddam Hussein didn't budge his troops, the Americans and thirty-three other nations formed a military coalition against him and moved in. This military operation, called Operation Desert Storm, involved the United States and its allies bombing strategic targets in Iraq, including the country's missile silos, command centers, and even Saddam Hussein's presidential palaces. It also involved a ground invasion, forcing the Iraqis to retreat from Kuwait. Within six weeks, Kuwait was liberated. Iraq was punished, but Saddam Hussein remained president. The brief clash was known as the Gulf War.

# The Case Against Saddam Hussein

In his State of the Union address on January 28, 2003, President Bush laid out his reasons why the United States should remove Saddam Hussein from power. Calling Saddam Hussein "a brutal dictator, with a history of reckless aggression, with ties to terrorism," Bush made his case why the Iraqi president posed a threat to the United States.[22] Saddam Hussein had agreed to destroy Iraq's weapons of mass destruction following the Gulf War, but Bush alleged that he had never done so. Saddam Hussein was said to have refused to cooperate with United Nations weapons inspectors who came to see proof of his efforts to disarm. Bush also asserted there was evidence that Saddam Hussein was building a nuclear bomb.

According to Bush, Saddam Hussein therefore represented a grave threat to national security. He also suggested the dictator had links to international terrorists. It was in America's best interest to stop Saddam Hussein before he launched a terrorist attack, he concluded. Bush was making the case for preventative war. He believed it was acceptable for the American military to strike first against an opponent that could potentially harm the United States, thereby preventing the deaths of innocent citizens. This reasoning became known as the

Bush doctrine. "We have no ambition in Iraq except to remove a threat and restore control of a country to its own people," Bush declared.[23] If the United States had to act alone or almost alone to remove the threat, it would.

## Invasion and Early Success

On Bush's orders, the United States began air strikes on the Iraqi capital, Baghdad, on March 19, 2003. The targets were mostly government buildings and Saddam Hussein's palaces. The bombs dropped from American airplanes turned "the target area into a cauldron of fireballs and drifting smoke," according to one report.[24]

Unlike during the Gulf War, where many countries contributed to forming a coalition that struck against Saddam Hussein, the United States was mostly acting alone this time. The United Nations refused to officially support the war. Some key American allies, including Germany and France, chose not to take part either. Nevertheless, American forces invading from the south advanced quickly through the country, meeting little resistance from the Iraqi military.

"We have no ambition in Iraq except to remove a threat and restore control of a country to its own people."[23]

– President George W. Bush, 2003

Five weeks later, it seemed to be over. After fighting several skirmishes with Saddam Hussein's Republican Guard as they swept through southern Iraq, American soldiers entered Baghdad on April 9. They received a hero's welcome from many Iraqis. Statues of Saddam Hussein were pulled from their pedestals as citizens celebrated their

Bush's speech under the "Mission Accomplished" banner was sharply criticized as the war dragged on. US troops would not withdraw from Iraq for another eight years.

liberation from his regime. Many people seemed delighted to be free of the dictator. "Touch me, touch me, tell me that this is real, tell me that the nightmare is really over," one observer exclaimed in delight as he watched the scenes of jubilation.[25]

Less than a month later, President Bush declared hostilities in Iraq were over. "The liberation of Iraq is a crucial advance in the campaign against terror," Bush said as he stood on the deck of the aircraft carrier USS *Abraham Lincoln* beneath a giant banner that read "Mission Accomplished." He continued: "We've removed an ally of al-Qaeda, and cut off a source of terrorist funding. And this much is certain: no terrorist network will gain weapons of mass destruction from the Iraqi regime, because that regime is no more."[26]

The next step, Bush announced, was to rebuild Iraq. Americans would transform Saddam Hussein's dictatorship into a democracy like the United States, whose leaders were elected by the people. Since doing that would require a military presence to keep the peace, the Americans would stay for the time being, he announced. In the meantime, the search for weapons of mass destruction and Saddam Hussein, who had vanished in the midst of the invasion, would continue.

## New Attacks, New Alarms

One of the first things the United States did was disband the Iraqi army. Although it was not immediately apparent, this was a large mistake that would come back to haunt the occupiers later. A quarter of a million men, still armed with their government-issued weapons, returned home to their villages without jobs or wages. They soon became restless. It wasn't long before some would turn their arms against the occupying American forces in an attempt to eject them from Iraq.

The American occupation had barely begun when the American coalition received a jarring warning that things were not as stable as they thought. In August 2003, a suicide bomber drove a truck packed with explosives into the side of a United Nations building in Baghdad. The truck exploded, toppling the building and leaving seventeen aid and relief workers dead. More than one hundred others were injured. The attack on the United Nations was a foretaste of things to come. During the next several months, guerrilla fighters attacked US soldiers again and again. They hurled bombs or improvised explosive devices at convoys. Occasionally, they engaged in suicide missions, blowing themselves up in crowded areas in hopes of killing Americans.

Between May and December 2003, 190 American soldiers died in such attacks. In the meantime, the search for both Saddam Hussein and his weapons of mass destruction continued. The first of those searches came to an end less than a year after the invasion. On December 13, the former dictator was discovered in a tiny crawl space on a farm near the village where he was born. The new government of Iraq put him on trial, convicted him of crimes against humanity, and sentenced him to death. He was executed in 2006.

Though Saddam Hussein's capture unleashed a wave of euphoria among the Iraqis who had suffered under his cruel rule, it did not make American occupation more tolerable to the citizens of Iraq. When Iraqi citizens defied intimidation from insurgents to vote in the country's first free elections in a generation in 2005, one young voter summed up the general feeling of the people. "Things will go right if people leave us alone to do what we want to do," he said. "If they leave the Iraqi people to decide for themselves, things will get better."[27]

**"Things will go right if people leave us alone to do what we want to do. If they leave the Iraqi people to decide for themselves, things will get better."[27]**

—An Iraqi voter on the future of his country, 2005

The weapons of mass destruction that Bush proclaimed Iraq possessed did not materialize. Instead of a nation fixated on developing nuclear weapons, in early 2004 CIA investigator David Kay described how the Iraqi system really worked. Kay found that scientists had asked Saddam Hussein for money for years, saying

## The *New York Times* and the Reasons for War

Much of the public evidence that Iraq possessed weapons of mass destruction came from reports published in the *New York Times* during the early 2000s. The *Times's* stories painted a picture of a nation that was trying to build a nuclear arsenal. But when reviewed under more intense scrutiny, many of the stories didn't hold up.

Information provided by one source, an Iraqi politician named Ahmed Chalabi, proved especially problematic when fact-checked. Chalabi and others sources had wanted Saddam Hussein out of power badly enough to exaggerate facts or lie to journalists about Iraq's supposed nuclear program. Their stories were published on the front pages of newspapers. Many politicians who read those newspapers eventually supported the decision to invade Iraq.

The errors were acknowledged by the newspaper's editors in an extraordinary editorial published in the *Times* in 2004. "Looking back, we wish we had been more aggressive in re-examining the claims as new evidence emerged—or failed to emerge," the newspaper's editors wrote. "Complicating matters for journalists, the accounts of these exiles were often eagerly confirmed by United States officials convinced of the need to intervene in Iraq. Administration officials now acknowledge that they sometimes fell for misinformation from these exile sources. So did many news organizations—in particular, this one."

"From the Editors; The Times and Iraq," New York Times, May 26, 2004. www.nytimes.com.

they were developing weapons. "Saddam was self-directing projects that were not vetted by anyone else. The scientists were able to fake programs," he concluded.[28] Once they had funding for their so-called nuclear projects, the scientists had spent the money on other things. Iraq had not been serious about developing nuclear weapons for more than a decade. Saddam Hussein's ignorance of science and his insistence on making major decisions alone had set him up to be duped, Kay said.

Additionally, there was no evidence for many of Bush's claims in his 2003 State of the Union address, including that Iraq was trying to import uranium, a key material in building nuclear weapons. The assertion that the White House was wrong about Saddam Hussein possessing weapons of mass destruction—the United States' main reason for invading Iraq—was deeply embarrassing to the Bush administration.

# Into the Heart of Insurgency

In March 2004, four Americans traveling through Fallujah, a city west of Baghdad, were ambushed by masked gunmen. The people of Fallujah seemed to think the dead were spies working for the CIA. The four men were not working for the US government but rather were employed by Blackwater Security Consulting, a private firm. It didn't matter: the men were killed, and their corpses were paraded through the streets by a joyful mob. Eventually, two were hung from a bridge over the Euphrates River as a jubilant crowd celebrated.

Fallujah had been a hotbed of death and chaos since the beginning of the conflict. American soldiers had killed several Iraqi civilians during a demonstration there in April 2003, and sixteen Americans had died when a helicopter was shot down outside the city several months later. The convoy of General John Abizaid, the highest-ranking US military official in the Middle East, had been attacked on the streets of Fallujah in February 2004. Though Abizaid was unharmed, these events made it clear what some Iraqis thought of Americans in their country.

Fallujah became the site of fierce fighting in the early years of the Iraq War. The US Marines played a central role for the American side in these battles.

Following the Blackwater deaths, US forces tried to take control of Fallujah. An offensive to regain the city, Operation Valiant Resolve, began on April 4, 2004. It was to be among the bloodiest battles of the Iraq War. American soldiers fought to flush out insurgents representing Saddam Hussein's Baathist Party and al Qaeda in a grim, street-by-street struggle in a city booby-trapped with IEDs. Bands of suicide-vest-clad insurgent fighters occupied buildings as the Americans laid siege. After ten days of intense fighting, the Americans gained the upper hand, though at great cost. Almost a hundred Americans were killed in battle, several hundred more were wounded, and the city of Fallujah was largely destroyed. The number of dead insurgents totaled more than 2,000.

Afterward, many wondered if the effort had been worth the cost. The purpose of having US forces in Iraq was to establish peace and to win the support of Iraqis through positive action. For them, would destroying Fallujah be looked on as a positive action in the long term? "What's the impact on a ten-year-old kid when he goes back and sees his neighborhood destroyed?" a colonel who had taken part in the battle mused. "And what is he going to do when he is 18 years old?"[29]

# Sunnis vs. Shias

The sun had barely risen over the golden dome of the al-Askari Shrine in Samarra, 60 miles (100 km) north of Baghdad, on February 22, 2006, when a dozen men in military uniforms burst in and took control of the building. The intruders set off a bomb in the famous golden dome, which collapsed into a heap of rubble. Word of the attack on one of the holiest sites in Shia Islam spread quickly throughout Iraq. Shias make up the majority of Muslims in Iraq. Adherents of the other major branch of Islam, Sunni Muslims, make up much of the remainder. The two sects have much in common but also have key differences in beliefs and traditions. The split originally came from a dispute in the 600s CE over which person was the rightful successor to Muhammad, the religion's founder.

Shias were deeply angered by the bombing of one of their greatest shrines. Before the day was over, Sunni mosques had been set on fire in retribution for the bombing. The headquarters of the main Sunni political party had been set on fire as well. The country was on edge. This was added to the insurgent violence against Americans

## The Photos That Shocked the World

The photographs that surfaced from the Abu Ghraib prison near Baghdad in April 2004 were brutal. There were bodies covered in human excrement. Photos showed dogs intimidating prisoners. Other images depicted prisoners being physically or sexually abused, all while American soldiers in charge of the prison stood by grinning and flashing thumbs-up signs.

What had happened here? A report written by General Antonio M. Taguba during the army's official investigation was damning. At Abu Ghraib, Taguba found, prisoners were subjected to "sadistic, blatant and wanton criminal abuses." President Bush denounced the soldiers' behavior at Abu Ghraib, but the damage was done. The photos inflamed public opinion against the soldiers who had perpetuated the atrocities. On the other side, seeing their American occupiers treat their own people this way helped sour relations between Iraqi civilians and US troops.

*Quoted in Seymour Hersh, "Torture at Abu Ghraib," New Yorker, May 10, 2004. www.newyorker.com.*

and violent acts against Shias by the Sunni organization al Qaeda in Iraq. The country seemed on the brink of civil war.

The US promise to rebuild the country and restore order seemed to be failing. With almost 3,000 American troops dead in the first three years of the war and little in the way of progress to show for it, American patience was running thin. Voters made their displeasure with the Bush administration clear during the 2006 midterm elections, when they voted key Republicans out of office. The results prompted Bush to accept the resignation of Defense Secretary Donald Rumsfeld, who had been one of the biggest supporters of the war. At the same time, insurgent violence continued to plague US troops and Iraqi civilians. The US military initiated a troop surge of 20,000

Americans early in 2007 to help bring stability to Baghdad and the Anbar Province, a center of Sunni insurgency. More American soldiers died in Iraq that year than in any other year since the war had begun.

Though public support for the war was waning in the United States, getting a handle on things in Iraq was imperative for American security, Bush argued. He said that the US should stay the course. "To step back now would force a collapse of the Iraqi government," Bush said. "Such a scenario would result in our troops being forced to stay in Iraq even longer, and confront an enemy that is even more lethal."[30]

Nevertheless, an agreement that provided a roadmap for the end of US operations in Iraq was announced in mid-November 2008. According to the agreement, most US forces would leave Iraq by mid-2009 and withdraw completely by 2012. As US convoys rolled south toward Kuwait in December 2011, insurgents hurled handmade bombs into their paths. Despite the official end to the war, many felt that leaving the Iraqi army to fend for itself against insurgents, al Qaeda, and other extremist Islamist groups was risky. Would the Iraqi army be able to withstand an insurgent threat? "From a standpoint of being able to defend against an external threat, they have very limited to little capability, quite frankly," remarked General Lloyd J. Austin III.[31]

# Violence Without Borders

Austin's theory was proven correct almost as soon as American troops left Iraq. The next two years were filled with insurgent fighting in what became known as the Iraq crisis. Fighting broke out along sectarian lines, with Sunnis attacking Shia members of the military and the police, notably with car bombs. Bombings rocked Baghdad and several other cities. A new group, spun off from al Qaeda and

The head of ISIS, Abu Bakr al-Baghdadi, appeared on video giving a speech from a Mosul mosque after his group took control of the city. Iraqi forces regained control of Mosul in 2017.

later known as the Islamic State in Iraq and Syria (ISIS), claimed responsibility for many of the bombings.

In June 2014, ISIS took things a step further. The group's militants attacked soldiers in Iraq's second-largest city, Mosul. The army fled, leaving ISIS in command of the city. "They took control of everything, and they are everywhere," one witness reported.[32] ISIS quickly imposed strict fundamentalist laws, forbidding music and making it obligatory for women to cover themselves in public. Its enemies, or perceived enemies, were beheaded on camera, and videos of the acts were leaked onto the internet. Iraqi prime minister Nouri al-Maliki called for help, but ISIS continued to consolidate its power over the northern part of the country. Fallujah, the city Americans fought so hard for in 2004, fell to ISIS a few months later.

In the United States, President Barack Obama weighed whether the United States should once again intervene in Iraq. The US government had previously given some weapons to the Iraqis, but much of the equipment later wound up in the hands of insurgents. In a report, the State Department labeled ISIS "not only a threat to the stability of Iraq, but a threat to the entire region."[33] The group's next objective was Baghdad, the capital city.

That summer, a small minority sect called the Yazidi fled into Iraq's Sinjar Mountains to escape persecution from ISIS. This situation helped make up Obama's mind. In August, he authorized humanitarian aid to the Yazidi, who were trapped in the mountains and dying of starvation. Additionally, the US military would carry out airstrikes that targeted ISIS convoys. American advisers and military experts were also dispatched to aid the Iraqi army. Obama said:

*When we face a situation like we do on that mountain—with innocent people facing the prospect of violence on a horrific scale, when we have a mandate to help—in this case, a request from the Iraqi government—and when we have the unique capabilities to help avert a massacre, then I believe the United States of America cannot turn a blind eye. We can act, carefully and responsibly, to prevent a potential act of genocide. That's what we're doing on that mountain.[34]*

But he was quick to add that a conflict like the one the United States had entered in 2003 would not happen again. "American combat troops will not be returning to fight in Iraq, because there's no American military solution to the larger crisis in Iraq," he said. "The only lasting solution is reconciliation among Iraqi communities and stronger Iraqi security forces."[35]

In the coming months, several other countries, including Belgium, France, Denmark, Morocco, the United Kingdom, and Australia, launched their own airstrikes at ISIS targets. The strikes, combined with the efforts of the Iraqi military on the ground, helped Iraq reclaim the strategic city of Mosul and the other territories of the so-called Islamic State in 2017.

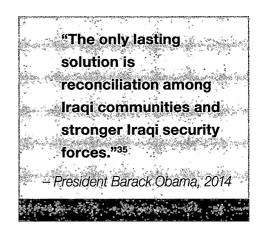

"The only lasting solution is reconciliation among Iraqi communities and stronger Iraqi security forces."[35]

— President Barack Obama, 2014

# The Impact of Iraq

The Bush administration's decision to stay in Iraq, to the point of committing thousands of troops to fight civilians who took up arms against the American occupiers, prolonged the conflict and led to tens of thousands of deaths. At the same time, it is impossible to know what would have happened had the Americans not intervened. Would the Iraqi people have been better off if Saddam Hussein had continued to be president?

Obama, in his 2014 speech authorizing airstrikes against ISIS, underlined that the United States cannot step in "every time there's a crisis in the world."[36] However, he also said that in a situation where Americans could help save lives, they should. Fighting in Iraq may not be over. Though weakened, many believe ISIS could rise again. Colonel Sean Ryan, a US military spokesman, put it this way in 2018: "As far as we are concerned, ISIS remains a threat as long as they have the capability to launch terror attacks anywhere, and we will pursue them until they are completely defeated."[37]

# Chapter 3

# What Is the Syrian Civil War?

The uprising began with a Tunisian fruit seller. Mohamed Bouazizi had struggled financially all his life. He did not make a lot of money, and since he did not have much education, he was unable to get a better job. Making things worse, Bouazizi's job made him vulnerable to run-ins with the corrupt local police. Policemen and market inspectors often harassed him, demanding money because Bouazizi did not have a seller's license. During one such run-in on December 17, 2010, a policewoman slapped and insulted him. Bouazizi's produce and cart were confiscated. Frustrated and dejected, Bouazizi went to a local government office to complain. He was turned away. He returned later that day, and this time he poured fuel over his body and set himself on fire in protest. Bouazizi died of his wounds two weeks later.

Bouazizi's desperate actions touched off a rush of anger and indignation that rippled through the Arab world. Throughout North Africa and the Middle East, men and women took to the streets in mass protests, demanding political reform and human rights from their governments. Explained one protester, "We are here because we want our dignity. We don't want to have to rely on political favors or bribes to get jobs; we need to clean out the system."[38] Thanks

Tunisians took to the streets to demand the release of protesters in January 2011. Other protests rippled across the Middle East as the Arab Spring spread.

to social media, information about protests spread quickly and galvanized participation. Within weeks, the governments of both Tunisia and Egypt had fallen from power.

In Syria too, the Arab Spring sparked protests against the government. There, however, the result was different. The Arab Spring was the precursor to an all-out civil war that has divided Syrians into warring factions, displaced millions of people, destroyed cities, and torn the country apart.

# The Government Against the People

For Syria, the decisive action happened in the town of Daraa. Emboldened by the Arab Spring uprisings that had led North African dictators to abdicate, someone had graffitied the words "It's your turn now, Doctor" on the wall of a local school. "Doctor" referred to Syrian president Bashar al-Assad, a trained eye doctor.[39]

Retribution came swiftly. Government agents working for Syrian security chief Atef Najib, who was also a cousin of Assad, woke Mouawiya Syasneh and fourteen other teenagers in their homes in the middle of the night. The teens were taken to a nearby police station and tortured until they confessed to spraying the graffiti.

The treatment of the adolescents shocked the local population. The people of Daraa marched in protest, demanding the government free the boys. Though they were eventually released, the government was determined to have the last word. The tanks of the Syrian army soon rolled into Daraa. The people of the city continued to protest, and people in nearby cities began protesting as well. The government showed little patience. In several cities, Assad's security forces opened fire or hurled tear-gas canisters on unarmed protesters, killing several citizens. It was March 2011. The protagonists of the conflict were still well-defined: the soldiers of a dictator versus the people demanding greater freedoms.

# The Houla Massacre

The government quickly showed that it could be ruthless in suppressing cities and villages suspected to be against Assad in any way. Security forces broke into homes and beat or even murdered citizens in front of their families. Following demonstrations in the village of Houla on May 25, 2012, the government fired artillery shells into neighborhoods. Afterward, a band of fighters supporting the government moved in and massacred entire families.

Videos of the bodies of ordinary citizens, including small children, shocked the world. The United Nations quickly condemned the act. The Houla Massacre spoiled a truce that had been in the works between the rebels and the government. The government blamed the attack on rebel "terrorists" who had taken up arms against the president and the Syrian army. Although it had been made clear what they were risking, the people of Houla continued to march in protest.

For more than a year, the story in Syria remained rebel fighters versus Assad's army. As in Houla, scores of people were killed for protesting as the army brutally repressed demonstrations with bullets and bombs. The rebels, including deserters from Assad's army, as well as armed civilians, began organizing themselves into groups. One group was the Free Syrian Army, which assassinated three of Assad's top security officials in a bomb attack in July 2012. As the government fought to regain control, rebels also took command of parts of Damascus, the nation's capital, and Aleppo, one of its largest cities.

A month later, Syria's prime minister, Riad Hijab, fled the country. "I have defected from the terrorist, murderous regime," he declared. "And I declare that from today I am a soldier of this holy revolution."[40] It was the first time Assad had suffered such public defeats, and analysts predicted the regime would clamp down even harder on the areas it still controlled. "The opposition has hit the jackpot," said one analyst, watching from London. "The consequences are too big to digest. It may provoke more violence by the regime. Everyone is revising their calculations."[41]

In August 2012, a burned-out tank sat in front of a destroyed mosque in Azaz, Syria. As the conflict raged, cities and civilians became collateral damage.

## Chemical Attack in Ghouta

In the early hours of August 21, 2013, Ghouta, a suburb of Damascus controlled by rebel fighters, was hit with rockets filled with the toxic nerve gas sarin. Sarin is a potentially lethal chemical weapon. This tasteless, colorless gas attacks the central nervous system after being inhaled. The attack was invisible but deadly. Victims begin foaming at the mouth and choking for breath. "It was like hell," remarked one observer. "The chemicals are silent. You don't know you're dying until you can smell it and then it is too late."[42]

The effects of the gas, documented on the internet in numerous videos of extremely sick people choking for air, broadcast the horror of what was happening in Syria. Once again, tragedy in Syria captured the world's attention. From Rome, Pope Francis addressed the crisis in remarks reflecting on the senselessness of war. "Nothing, but nothing can justify the use of such instruments of extermination on defenseless people," the Pope said.[43]

Hundreds of people died in the gas attack in Ghouta. While the Syrian government is largely assumed to have been responsible for the disaster, Assad's government denied it. Afterward, however, the government did give up what it said were all of its chemical weapons to be destroyed by United Nations forces. Unfortunately, Ghouta was not the last chemical weapons attack Syrians would face.

> "It was like hell. The chemicals are silent. You don't know you're dying until you can smell it and then it is too late."[42]
>
> – An observer on chemical attacks against the Syrian people

# ISIS Joins the Fight

One particular group watched the civil war unfold in Syria with keen interest. Al Qaeda, the Islamic extremist group established by Osama bin Laden during the 1980s, saw in Syria an opportunity to accomplish a long-held goal. Al Qaeda had long wanted establish an Islamic state where people lived strictly according to sharia, or Islamic law. In 2011, months after Bin Laden was killed by American military forces, the organization's new leader in Iraq authorized

Abu Mohammad al-Golani to form a new branch of al Qaeda in Syria. In one way at least, Golani's mission was aligned with the antigovernment rebels: both wanted to end Assad's rule over the country.

Golani quickly got to work. Once inside Syria, he met up with former inmates of the dreaded Sednaya military prison who had been released by Assad in the early days of the conflict in 2011. Assad had released the prisoners as a way of showing the people he was conceding to their demands. The prisoners were all Islamic fundamentalists eager to create an Islamic state. Some had fought for al Qaeda in Iraq. Golani and his new comrades called their group Jabhat al-Nusra l'Ahl as-Sham, meaning "Support Front for the People of the Sham." *Sham* is a word for Syria and the surrounding region. The group was known as the Nusra Front for short.

The Nusra Front quickly distinguished itself as one of the more effective rebel forces among the many groups that had formed. These groups also included the Free Syrian Army, which lacked the powerful weapons needed to really make an impact, and an organization called the Army of Conquest that would form later. At the Battle of Raqqa in March 2013, the Nusra Front showed its strength. Aided by other rebel groups, the front captured a provincial governor and gained control of much of Raqqa, a northern city.

At first, the Nusra Front enjoyed widespread support from the rebels, who rallied behind it after the United States condemned it as a terrorist organization in 2012. Few people knew that Nusra was really part of al Qaeda in Iraq. The news became public in April 2013 when Abu Bakr al-Baghdadi, the leader of al Qaeda in Iraq, announced that the two groups would henceforth be a single group: ISIS, or the Islamic State of Iraq and Syria. Ayman al-Zawahiri, who controlled the original al Qaeda following Bin Laden's death, protested combining

Vast numbers of civilians, including many children, were displaced by the conflict in Syria. They sought shelter in refugee camps.

the two groups. After that, Baghdadi and his supporters became ISIS, still with the goal of establishing a transnational Islamic state. The few who supported Golani remained with the Nusra Front, which remained loyal to Zawahiri and al Qaeda.

From then on, the Nusra Front and ISIS opposed each other for control in Syria. They joined a growing number of groups all fighting for control in a Syria coming apart at the seams. In the west, Hezbollah, a Lebanon-based group supporting the Syrian government, committed arms and fighters to battling the rebels. The Army of Conquest, which came to prominence in 2015, supported the rebels and declared itself against Hezbollah.

Among them all, ISIS soon gained the upper hand. In June 2014, Baghdadi declared the establishment of the long-awaited Islamic State under a black flag. The new Islamic State stretched from Aleppo throughout the northern part of the country and into Iraq. Baghdadi was announced as its caliph, or leader.

ISIS quickly became known for its extreme tactics, even when compared to other extremist groups like al Qaeda. While Bin Laden had tried to justify his actions as reasonable because of American actions in the Middle East, Baghdadi simply used violence without trying to rationalize it. ISIS enforced strict sharia law over the territories it controlled, forbidding smoking, drinking, and even music as unholy pleasures. Women were expected to stay at home and dress modestly. If they didn't, they risked being whipped. Those who violated the law or opposed ISIS in any way would be killed, often by being beheaded.

ISIS soldiers also took women and girls as slaves and indiscriminately shot those who tried to flee war-torn cities. These new developments horrified human rights groups. "Shooting children as they try to run to safety with their families—there are no words of condemnation strong enough for such despicable acts," remarked Zeid Ra'ad Al Hussein, the United Nations High Commissioner for Human Rights. The group's attacks on innocent, unarmed citizens, he added, amounted to "war crimes."[44]

# Russia, Turkey, and Iran Lend A Hand

After having committed a lot of money and manpower to conflicts in both Iraq and Afghanistan, the United States was at first hesitant to intervene in Syria with combat troops. The extremism of ISIS and its affiliations with al Qaeda in Iraq, however, were enough to convince President Obama to take action. With support from Bahrain, Jordan, Saudi Arabia, and the United Arab Emirates, the United States bombed ISIS strongholds in Raqqa and the cities around it beginning in August 2014. Though dozens of ISIS fighters were killed

## Refugee Crisis

Fatima and her children were living in Daraa when the Shabiha, a militia loyal to Assad, broke into her apartment one night. "They accused my husband of being part of the opposition," she recalled. "He wasn't." As Fatima and her children watched, her husband was raped and beaten by the Shabiha, then thrown out the window. He died from his wounds.

Rami, an emergency medical technician, left Aleppo after falling under suspicion for providing medical care to both government and opposition forces. "My only crime was that I was helping people," he said.[2] The violence that has defined the Syrian Civil War caused Fatima, Rami, and thousands of Syrians like them to flee their homes and villages.

More than 5 million Syrians have gone abroad seeking asylum as refugees. Another 6 million are estimated to have left their homes for other parts of Syria. Some crossed into neighboring countries of Jordan, Lebanon, and Turkey. Others made harrowing journeys in overcrowded rafts to Greece, the gateway to other parts of Europe. The influx of thousands of refugees, however, has strained the capacities of governments who are still struggling to find solutions about what to do with so many displaced people.

1. Quoted in Bassam S. Rifai, "Syrian Refugees Tell Their Harrowing Stories in Their Own Words," New York Daily News, September 13, 2015. www.nydailynews.com.

2. Quoted in Patrick McDonnell, "A Desperate Migration," LA Times, September 18, 2015. www.latimes.com.

in the attacks, women and children caught in the crossfire were killed as well.

Initially, the war had been about government troops and antigovernment rebels opposing each other. The new dimension of the civil war now involved battling ISIS as well. In addition to the United States, Russian and Syrian government forces also began actively working together to defeat ISIS. During 2015 and 2016, one contested area was the ancient city of Palmyra, a site of significant archeological importance. Palmyra was captured by ISIS in 2015, and the fighters proceeded to dynamite important sites and destroy many of its historically valuable monuments, particularly the ones from the Roman period before the rise of Islam. Many saw the damage as senseless. "It is worth pointing out that earlier Muslims who have occupied Palmyra didn't see fit to destroy it," the British newspaper the *Guardian* remarked. "ISIS is erasing, then, not just pre-Islamic culture, but Islamic heritage, too."[45]

The struggle for Palmyra was fraught and contentious. With help from the Russians, Assad's government forces were able to wrest the city back from ISIS in the spring of 2016, only to lose it again at the end of the year. Russia had first emerged as an ally of the Syrian government in 2012, when international observers discovered it was providing Assad's soldiers with weapons. By 2015, it was actively aiding the Assad government as it struggled against ISIS in Aleppo, Syria's biggest city, and against rebel groups in other parts of the country.

By 2016, Turkey, Syria's neighbor to the north, was involved too. Turkish troops entered Syria to help rebels defeat ISIS near the Turkish border. Slowly, the combined forces recaptured territory that had been held by ISIS. As 2016 concluded, a combination of government

The Russian military launched airstrikes against ISIS from bases in Syria. It worked alongside the Syrian government to help the Assad regime maintain control over the country.

troops, the Russian air force, and militias sponsored by Iran, another ally of Assad, retook Aleppo. Losing the city was a huge blow to ISIS.

With aid from Russia and Turkey, the Syrian government forces slowly turned the tide against ISIS. The Islamic State was driven out of Raqqa in October 2017. In November, the Syrian army retook Deir al-Zour, another strategic city. One month after that, Russian president Vladimir Putin visited Syria, where he declared the joint Russian-Syrian government effort victorious. Russia, Turkey, and Iran also agreed to enforce a cease-fire between the government's forces and the rebels.

# The Ongoing War

Expelling ISIS from Syria did not halt the civil war. Once back in control of the land, the Syrian government reverted to its old ways. Government troops continued terrorizing the population with chemical weapons. After a chemical attack killed more than eighty civilians in 2017, President Donald Trump authorized a missile strike on an airfield in the Homs province of western Syria where the chemical attack had been launched from. Trump defended the decision as being vital to national security. "Years of previous attempts at changing Assad's behavior have all failed, and failed very dramatically," he said. "As a result, the refugee crisis continues to deepen, and the region continues to destabilize, threatening the United States and its allies."[46]

Though the Syrian government, still aided by Russia and Iran, seemed to have regained power and control in much of the country by 2018, atrocities were still being committed against the Syrian people. "Sadly, the enduring violence in these areas has not changed in nature," human rights scholar Paulo Sérgio Pinheiro reported to the United Nations Human Rights Council. "Violence continues to be directed against civilians, with complete disrespect for civilian protection. . . . Whether it be the unrestrained use of airstrikes against residential neighbourhoods, attacks against doctors and hospitals, or the use of suicide bombers that deliberately target civilians, fighting remains brutal in purpose and reprehensible in method."[47]

The year 2018 brought fresh horrors to the civilian population that remains in Syria. There was another chemical attack on Ghouta, still a rebel stronghold, where the bombs fell "like rain," as one eyewitness reported.[48] The attack left many there who had lived through the 2013 sarin attacks with a disquieting sense of familiarity. Once again, the United States, France, and the United Kingdom responded by bombing government targets.

At the beginning of 2019, more than half a million people were estimated to have been killed in the eight-year civil war. Fully half of Syria's 22 million people had been forced to leave their homes. An estimated 5 million became refugees, with thousands still living in refugee camps in the Middle East. Of those who stayed, approximately 60 percent live in extreme poverty, as war disrupts the national economy and normal life. Many of Syria's proud cities, some of which had stood for more than 1,000 years, have been bombed to the ground.

> "Years of previous attempts at changing Assad's behavior have all failed, and failed very dramatically. As a result, the refugee crisis continues to deepen, and the region continues to destabilize, threatening the United States and its allies."[46]
>
> – President Donald Trump, 2017

In December 2018, President Trump announced that he would be pulling out the 2,000 American combat troops currently in the country. "We have defeated ISIS in Syria," the president tweeted.[49] American reactions to this announcement were mixed. Some feared that withdrawing US troops could spur an ISIS resurgence. Others felt that ISIS had been sufficiently weakened, and that the United States should leave Syria to sort itself out. Eight years after the government began firing on demonstrators, the fate of the country remained unclear.

# Chapter 4

# Where Else Have Terror and War Happened?

The long, drawn-out conflicts in Afghanistan, Iraq, and Syria have dominated the international headlines of the early part of the twenty-first century. At the same time, technology has made the world smaller, allowing viewers to watch history as it is livestreamed on the internet. Military innovations have provided nations like the United States the power to intervene by dropping missiles on strategic targets literally half a world away.

Though Afghanistan, Iraq, and Syria have received the lion's share of news coverage during the past few decades, they are not the only places where war and terrorism have harmed people. This chapter looks at some of the other conflicts around the globe that have shaped the cultural and political climate in their regions and cut deeply into the fabric of local societies, dramatically changing the lives of citizens involved.

## Ukraine

Ukraine's story began with protests against the government. The country was on the verge of a historic free-trade agreement with

Vladimir Putin sought to keep Ukraine within Russia's influence, rather than seeing it join the European Union. Putin has played a role in several conflicts and controversies of the twenty-first century, including the war in Syria.

the European Union (EU). Many Ukrainians supported the deal, which would have modernized the country's struggling economic and political systems and brought Ukraine closer to the EU. Russia, however, opposed the deal. The Russian government, led by President Vladimir Putin, pressured Ukraine to sign its own agreement, along with Belarus and Kazakhstan. Ukraine had to choose, Russian officials insisted. "Signing this agreement about association with EU, the Ukrainian government violates the treaty on strategic partnership and friendship with Russia," remarked Sergei Glazyev, one of Putin's advisors.[50]

The threat was clear: if certain pro-Russian parts of Ukraine, notably those in the eastern part of the country, appealed to Russia for help, Russia would be compelled to annex them from Ukraine. Caught between two powers, with the EU on one side and Russia on the other, President Viktor Yanukovych yielded to Russia. The deal with the EU hinged on releasing former Ukrainian Prime Minister Yulia Tymoshenko, Yanukovych's biggest political rival, from prison. When the Ukrainian parliament threw out legislation allowing Tymoshenko's release, the EU deal was suspended. Bullying by Russia, which had threatened to hurt Ukraine's economy if it signed with the EU, was largely seen as the cause.

Ukrainians took to the streets in protest, clashing with state police throughout the winter. Things escalated in the capital city of Kiev on February 20, 2014. Protestors in Independence Square began by throwing rocks and Molotov cocktails at police, and gunfire was exchanged. Dozens were killed. In the aftermath, the government and the protesters blamed each other for the violence.

In the meantime, the protests spread to other cities, particularly in the western parts of the country, which tended to be more pro-Europe. Meanwhile, police officers from western Ukraine left their posts and joined protesters, a sign that the government was losing control of its own forces. "We want to make a statement that we cannot tolerate what's going on anymore," one commander explained. "We want to show everyone that the police is with the people."[51]

Faced with the potential of his own forces deserting him, Yanukovych fled Kiev on February 22. Tymoshenko was released from prison the same day. At a rally in Independence Square, she called Yanukovych a dictator. "You were able to change Ukraine, and you can do everything," she told the protesters. "Everyone has a right to take part in building a European, independent state."[52]

Not everyone was pleased by the protesters' stand in Kiev, however. In the southern part of the country, where many ethnic Russians lived, people took to the street to protest Yanukovych's flight. In early March, Russian troops quietly moved into the Crimean Peninsula, a region of southern Ukraine on the Black Sea where many ethnic Russians lived. While Putin claimed that Russia had the right to protect the interests of the Russians in the region, US Secretary of State John Kerry denounced the move as an occupation.

Three weeks later, Russia officially annexed the peninsula. The move caused international outcry, though not in Russia, where Putin and many others saw it as a natural coming together of Russian people who had been separated by the breakup of the Soviet Union. "Crimea has always been an integral part of Russia in the hearts and minds of people," Putin said at a rally in Moscow after the news was announced.[53] In Crimea, regional officials organized a referendum, a vote on a single issue, about whether the region should attach itself to Russia. Following the election, officials announced that 97 percent of the voters approved the measure. Many in the West doubted the credibility of the referendum.

The annexation spurred some Russia supporters living in eastern Ukraine to take up arms against the Ukrainian government. These soldiers took control of a smattering of government buildings and

> "You were able to change Ukraine, and you can do everything. Everyone has a right to take part in building a European, independent state."[52]
>
> – Former Ukrainian Prime Minister Yulia Tymoshenko to Ukrainian protesters

airports in eastern Ukraine, prompting the Ukrainian government to send its national guard into the region. Watching from Russia, Putin warned that the country was on the brink of civil war. Throughout the next several months, both sides refused to back down. In the east, the people in the regions around the cities Donetsk and Luhansk declared themselves the Donetsk and Luhansk People's Republics, respectively. Following several violent skirmishes with government forces, a ceasefire between the groups was declared in September 2014. But violence broke out again in the following months, including one incident that destroyed the airport in Donetsk. A new ceasefire was proclaimed in 2015.

The deal between Ukraine and the EU that sparked the conflict was signed in June 2014, but it did not end the violence, which flared up sporadically in the years that followed. Both Russia and Ukraine have suffered for their actions. Ukraine's economy declined as a result of the violence and the annexation of Crimea. The fighting in the Donetsk and Luhansk regions, which are rich in coal, led to a coal shortage that threatened the company's electrical resources and forced rolling blackouts. More than 10,000 people are estimated to have died in the conflict. Russia's actions in Crimea led NATO to impose sanctions on the country, hurting the Russian economy. The Russian ruble declined in value compared to other currencies, which contributed to an economic recession.

# Nigeria

The headlines—explaining that schoolgirls had been kidnapped at gunpoint by a radical Islamist group—were chilling. In Chibok, Nigeria, in April 2014, 276 female students at a boarding school disappeared, taken away by a deadly terrorist organization. Al Qaeda in Iraq and

The militant group Boko Haram exploded a bomb in Maiduguri, Nigeria, in the summer of 2015. Bomb attacks and kidnappings made the group infamous.

Afghanistan, the Taliban in Pakistan, and more recently ISIS in Iraq and Syria have all aimed to establish an Islamic state where the people obey strict sharia law. In Nigeria, Boko Haram had the same goal. Founded in 2002 by Islamic cleric Mohammed Yusuf as a religious institution, Boko Haram initially provided Muslims with an alternative to the schools established by the British in Nigeria during the twentieth century. The group's official name was "People Committed to the Propagation of the Prophet's Teachings and Jihad," but locals eventually began calling it Boko Haram, which loosely translates as "Western education is forbidden."

Over time, Yusuf began advocating for holy war. His school became a training ground for soldiers in this planned conflict. In July 2009, the group began to make its presence felt. In what became known as the Boko Haram uprising, the organization rampaged through the city of Maiduguri, destroying buildings and wreaking havoc in an attack that killed several hundred people. Nigerian state police responded by raiding the group's headquarters complex and executing more than one hundred Boko Haram members, including many who were cornered inside the group's mosque. Yusuf was captured and died in Nigerian police custody, and responsibility for Boko Haram transferred to his lieutenant Abubakar Shekau.

The group was responsible for several vicious and violent attacks between 2009 and 2012, including one on the United Nations compound in the capital Abuja, where a car bomb killed twenty-three people. In 2012, Boko Haram blew up the police headquarters and several government buildings in Kano, Nigeria's second-largest city. Police also discovered cars packed with explosives and IEDs hidden in objects like soda cans scattered throughout the city. For all that, it wasn't until members donned military uniforms and set up a fake checkpoint where travelers were trapped and killed in 2013 that the US State Department labeled Boko Haram a foreign terrorist organization.

More than 2 million Nigerians have fled their homes in an attempt to escape Boko Haram, fearing capture or worse. The Nigerian military has had mixed results in fighting Boko Haram and reclaiming territory. Some citizens have said that in fighting the insurgents, the military has committed atrocities against civilians as well. In 2017, thinking it was attacking Boko Haram, the military mistakenly bombed a camp of people who had fled their homes, killing nearly one hundred innocent people.

In 2014 came the kidnapping of the girls from Chibok. Though not the first time that Boko Haram had kidnapped children, something about the Chibok girls stood out. Perhaps it was the photo released showing the girls in captivity, sitting close together wearing long robes and looking frightened and downcast. "It was the articulation of this whole saga," commented Saudatu Mahdi, who helped found the Bring Back Our Girls movement in Nigeria. "They became a rallying point."[54]

## Malala Yousafzai

All Malala Yousafzai wanted was an education. But it wasn't easy being a female student in Mingora, Pakistan, in the early 2000s. Taliban extremists had risen to power and controlled the Swat Valley, where her family lived. The Taliban banned music and forbade girls from going to school. Fortunately for Malala, her father ran a girls' school and believed in a woman's right to study, even if the Taliban didn't.

For years, Malala and her classmates defied the Taliban and courageously attended classes. In addition, she spoke up for a woman's right to an education, penning a column from her perspective for a British news website. Advocating for women's rights made her famous, but it also made her a target. In 2012, the Taliban sought her out. A gunman entered the school bus she was riding in with other children, then shot the fifteen-year-old in the head.

Malala's life was saved through an international medical effort that extended from Pakistan to the United Kingdom, where her family now lives. The story of her persistence and determination in the face of a terrorist group who would deny her and her gender the right to an education has been widely celebrated. Recovered from the shooting, Malala has dedicated herself to speaking out for the rights of girls and children everywhere, and she stands out as a fierce advocate of education. In 2014, she was awarded the Nobel Peace Prize.

While in captivity with Boko Haram, the women were forced to act as wives, cooking and cleaning and aiding their captors. Several eventually gave birth. Others who refused to sleep with group members became unwilling suicide bombers. These young women had bombs strapped to their bodies and were dropped off in crowded areas. "They told me to go to the big mosque and sit among the worshippers," one recalled.[55] She walked to a police station instead, where officers helped her.

Then, over a period of about a year beginning in 2016, an extraordinary thing happened: Boko Haram set groups of the kidnapped schoolgirls free. Many who were kidnapped eventually returned to their families and their normal lives, though they bear the emotional scars of their ordeals. Those who have been released or who escaped have received counseling and have had the opportunity to learn English and other subjects at a Western-style school, exactly the sort of institution that Boko Haram despises. In the meantime, others have been kidnapped. Following another mass abduction in 2018, the Nigerian Air Force was deployed to search for the missing girls from the air. It was clear that Boko Haram remained a serious threat in Nigeria.

# Yemen

Like those in other Arab nations, Yemenis were deeply moved by the Arab Spring that swept across North Africa and the Middle East in 2011. Dissatisfied with their own government and President Ali Abdullah Saleh, antigovernment forces aimed to oust him. At a protest called the Friday of Dignity on March 18, 2011, armed gunmen with military rifles killed dozens of protesters. The killings only added fuel to the fire. When army general Ali Mohsen threw his support to

Fighting in Yemen has created a catastrophic humanitarian crisis. Homes, businesses, and infrastructure lay in ruins.

the protesters later that year, Saleh agreed to step down. His vice president, Abdu Rabbu Mansour Hadi, took control of the country. In the meantime, Yemen was dealing with its local branch of al Qaeda, known as "al Qaeda in the Arabian Peninsula," which unleashed chaos with suicide bomber attacks on the population.

In northern Yemen, meanwhile, another antigovernment force was at work. While the government was occupied with al Qaeda, another rebel movement brought large sections of northern Yemen under its control. This movement was known as Ansar Allah, or the Houthi force after founder Hussein Badreddin al-Houthi. The Houthi rebels surprised everyone by taking control of the capital Sanaa in September 2014. President Hadi resigned less than four months later, and the Houthi leadership announced the government had been dissolved until further notice.

Hadi fled the country, but the field was not left clear for the Houthis. As Hadi exited, Saudi Arabia threw its support behind him and launched airstrikes on Yemen in order to try to get him back in power. The Saudi Arabian government said it was getting involved "to protect Yemen and his dear people from the aggression of the Houthi militias which were and are still a tool in the hands of foreign powers that don't stop meddling with the security and stability of brotherly Yemen."[56] Saudi involvement in turn angered Iran, another major player in Middle Eastern politics. The two nations distrusted each other, with Saudi Arabia accusing Iran of secretly backing the Houthis. In 2015, the Houthis and the Saudis went to war. The Saudis' goal was to restore Hadi as president. The Houthis, meanwhile, enjoyed the support of Saleh, the former dictator.

For the people of Yemen, the war has been a disaster. Fighting on the ground, coupled with airstrikes from the Saudi-led alliance, has turned what was already a bad situation in the Middle East's poorest country into a nightmare for its citizens. Many of the Saudi airstrikes have fallen in populated neighborhoods, killing thousands of innocent civilians. In addition, many Yemenis are living in dire circumstances, with more than a million children malnourished or risking death from starvation.

In 2018, a full 80 percent of Yemeni citizens were thought to be living in poverty. A cholera epidemic and poor sanitation in urban areas have exacerbated the crisis. "It is the largest humanitarian crisis in the world," according to one aid worker.[57] "People in Yemen are dying today not just because of the bullets and bombs, but because they are unable to receive the medical care they need to stay alive," echoed Dr. Ahmed Al-Mandhari, who oversees the World Health Organization's efforts in the Eastern Mediterranean.[58] Meanwhile, neither of the opposing sides in the civil war has been able to deal the other a definitive defeat.

> "People in Yemen are dying today not just because of the bullets and bombs, but because they are unable to receive the medical care they need to stay alive."[58]
>
> —Dr. Ahmed Al-Mandhari, who oversees the World Health Organization's efforts in the Eastern Mediterranean

# Terrorist Attacks Around the World

During the early twenty-first century, the frequency of terrorist attacks around the globe has risen, disrupting civilian life in normally peaceful areas. The easy availability of guns and other weapons, combined with the spread of terrorist ideals on social media, has had a deadly impact on dozens of occasions.

In the United States, several bombers and shooters have allegedly been inspired by the actions of international extremist groups, including al Qaeda and the Islamic State. Among the incidents caused by these terrorists was a bombing of the Boston Marathon on April 15, 2013. Two bombs concealed in backpacks exploded near the race's finish line in downtown Boston, Massachusetts. The blasts killed three, including an eight-year-old boy, and injured more than 250 others. There was mass panic as spectators fled the blasts, with some stopping to help the injured.

A manhunt for the suspected perpetrators, brothers Tamerlan and Dzhokhar Tsarnaev, was launched four days later. While Tamerlan was killed by police, his brother was found hiding in a boat. Dzhokhar was convicted of thirty federal charges and sentenced to death. Though unconnected with any terrorist groups, they were said to be influenced by radical Islamic beliefs.

In Orlando, Florida, on June 12, 2016, a man named Omar Mateen walked into Pulse, a gay nightclub, carrying an assault rifle and a pistol. Once inside, he opened fire. Mateen took the lives of forty-nine people in the deadliest terrorist attack on US soil since September 11, 2001. After a standoff that lasted more than three hours, Mateen was killed by police. Afterward, it was discovered that he had pledged allegiance to the Islamic State.

The alarming trend of mass shootings in public areas and at public events has shaken the American population to its core. The occurrences have also led to public demonstrations calling for greater restrictions on who can purchase guns and what kinds of weapons should be banned by law.

# France

The year 2015 was difficult for the people of France. In January, armed gunmen Saïd and Chérif Kouachi entered the offices of satirical newspaper *Charlie Hebdo* in Paris and killed twelve noted journalists and editors, including four of France's most celebrated political cartoonists. They also killed a policeman in the building. The Kouachi brothers fled the site of the massacre and ran through the streets of Paris brandishing their weapons before coming into contact with more police. Another police officer was killed, and the brothers again escaped. In the following days, a third gunman killed a policewoman

Los Angeles residents demonstrated in front of a French restaurant following the attack in Paris. People around the world expressed solidarity with the victims of the murders.

and four shoppers in a Jewish supermarket. Police stormed the store and killed the shooter.

The manhunt for the brothers came to an end two days later after French special forces surrounded a building northeast of Paris where they were hiding. Al Qaeda on the Arabian Peninsula, a terrorist organization based in Yemen, claimed responsibility for the attack. The shooting at the newspaper's offices triggered a national outpouring of support for journalism. Proclaiming solidarity and a commitment to freedom, the hashtag #JeSuisCharlie ("I am Charlie") gained traction on social media. In recognition of the tragedy, the Eiffel Tower briefly went dark.

In November of the same year, Paris was shaken again by a coordinated series of attacks that targeted several sites, including the Stade de France football stadium, where a soccer match attended by French president François Hollande was underway. Three suicide bombers blew themselves up outside the stadium, while diners in the cafés and restaurants in the popular République quarter were targeted by gunmen and a suicide bomber. At the Bataclan club and concert venue not far from République, gunmen entered the club and opened fire during a rock concert, sparking a panic inside. One hundred and thirty people lost their lives on this night of terror.

# Norway

A terrorist attack carried out in Oslo, the capital city of Norway, by a thirty-two-year-old Norwegian man was the worst in the country since World War II and stunned the world. People wondered how this could happen in Norway, a neutral, peaceful Scandinavian country noted for its high quality of life and thought to be far removed from violent political conflicts.

Anders Behring Breivik, a Norwegian with extreme right-wing political views, orchestrated the attack on the capital city, placing a bomb that damaged a tall government building on July 22, 2011. The explosion killed seven people and rained debris onto the surrounding area. Wearing a police officer's uniform, Breivik next went to the nearby island of Utoya, where he gained access to a summer camp and opened fire. The camp was affiliated with a left-wing political party. Breivik killed sixty-nine people, most of them teenagers.

Breivik was captured by police and demonstrated himself to be unrepentant about his actions. In court, he deliberately performed a Nazi salute and said he would have liked to have killed more people. He received the maximum prison sentence from a Norwegian court—twenty-one years—for carrying out the massacre, though it is likely that extensions to the sentence will keep Breivik imprisoned for the rest of his life.

# War and Terror in the Twenty-First Century

"It is much harder to build peace than it is to destroy it," Steve Killelea, chairman and founder of the Institute for Economics and Peace, commented in 2018.[59] The proliferation of violent attacks perpetrated by one or more individuals or groups, capable of killing dozens or even hundreds of people at a time, bears out his statement. The wars of the twenty-first century in the Middle East and elsewhere have caused the deaths of millions of people and the displacement of millions more, as terror attacks have also brought the violence of war to civilian populations. It is up to world leaders, governments, and individual communities to find ways to stop the violence. Doing so remains one of the great challenges of our age.

> **"It is much harder to build peace than it is to destroy it."[59]**
>
> *—Steve Killelea, chairman and founder of the Institute for Economics and Peace, 2018*

# SOURCE NOTES

## Introduction: An American Nightmare

1. Quoted in David Friend, *Watching the World Change: The Stories Behind the Images of 9/11*. New York: Farrar, Straus & Giroux, 2006. p. 189.

2. Quoted in Michael Ellison, Ed Vulliamy, and Jane Martinson, "We Got Down to the Outside and It Was Like an Apocalypse," *Guardian*, September 12, 2001. www.theguardian.com.

3. George W. Bush, "Remarks at Emma Booker Elementary School," *American Rhetoric*, n.d. www.americanrhetoric.com.

4. Quoted in Michael Powell, "In 9/11 Chaos, Giuliani Forged a Lasting Image," *New York Times*, September 21, 2007. www.nytimes.com.

5. "Address to a Joint Session of Congress and the American People," *The White House*, September 2001. http://georgewbush-whitehouse.archives.gov.

## Chapter 1: What Happened in Afghanistan and the War on Terror?

6. Quoted in Kate Zernike and Michael T. Kaufman, "The Most Wanted Face of Terrorism," *New York Times*, May 2, 2011. www.nytimes.com.

7. Quoted in "Wrath of God," *Time*, January 11, 1999. www.time.com.

8. Quoted in Chris Whipple, "What the CIA Knew Before 9/11: New Details," *Politico*, November 14, 2015. www.politico.eu.

9. Quoted in Elaine Sciolino, "After the Attacks: The Overview; Long Battle Seen," *New York Times*, September 15, 2001. www.nytimes.com.

10. James Barron, "Thousands Feared Dead as World Trade Center Is Toppled," *New York Times*, September 11, 2001. www.nytimes.com.

11. "Address to a Joint Session of Congress and the American People," *The White House*, September 2001. http://georgewbush-whitehouse.archives.gov.

12. "Address to a Joint Session of Congress and the American People."

13. "Address to a Joint Session of Congress and the American People."

14. Quoted in Steven Erlanger and John Kifner, "A Nation Challenged: The Politics; Afghan Talks Stall in Bonn on Comments from Kabul," *New York Times*, December 1, 2001. www.nytimes.com.

15. Quoted in "Taliban Fighters Storm US Base," *Al Jazeera*, July 14, 2008. www.aljazeera.com.

16. Quoted in Bill Gertz, "US Ignored Warnings Before Deadly Afghan Attack," *Washington Times*, October 16, 2009. www.washingtontimes.com.

17. Quoted in Barbara Starr, "Obama Approves Afghanistan Troop Increase," *CNN Politics*, February 18, 2009. www.cnn.com.

18. Quoted in Ewen MacAskill and Patrick Wintour, "Afghanistan Withdrawal: Barack Obama Says 33,000 Troops Will Leave Next Year," *Guardian*, June 22, 2011. www.theguardian.com.

19. "NATO Secretary General's Statement on a New Chapter in Afghanistan," *NATO*, December 28, 2014. www.nato.int.

20. Krishnadev Calamur, "No End in Sight," *Atlantic*, September 11, 2018. www.theatlantic.com.

## Chapter 2: What Happened in the Iraq War?

21. Michael R. Gordon and Eric Schmitt, "Vigilance and Memory: The Military; Move to Gulf by Key Unit Could Set Staff for Iraq War," *New York Times*, September 12, 2002. www.nytimes.com.

22. "Text of President Bush's 2003 State of the Union Address," *Washington Post*, January 28, 2003. www.washingtonpost.com.

23. Quoted in David E. Sanger and John F. Burns, "Threats and Responses: The White House; Bush Orders Start of War on Iraq; Missiles Apparently Miss Hussein," *New York Times*, March 20, 2003. www.nytimes.com.

24. John F. Burns, "A Nation at War: Baghdad; A Staggering Blow Strikes at the Heart of the Iraqi Capital," *New York Times*, March 22, 2003. www.nytimes.com.

25. Quoted in John F. Burns, "A Nation at War: Tumult; Cheers, Tears and Looting in Capital's Streets," *New York Times*, April 10, 2003. www.nytimes.com.

26. Quoted in "A Crucial Advance in the Campaign Against Terror," *Guardian*, May 1, 2003. www.theguardian.com.

27. Quoted in Dexter Filkins, "Defying Threats, Millions of Iraqis Flock to Polls," *New York Times*, January 31, 2005. www.nytimes.com.

28. Quoted in James Risen, "The Struggle for Iraq: Intelligence; Ex-Inspector Says CIA Missed Disarray in Iraqi Arms Program," *New York Times*, January 26, 2004. www.nytimes.com.

29. Quoted in James A. Warren, "The Vicious Battle to Capture Fallujah in 2004 Was a Close Fought Nightmare," *Daily Beast*, July 16, 2016. www.thedailybeast.com.

30. Quoted in David E. Sanger, "Bush Adds Troops in Bid to Secure Iraq," *New York Times*, January 11, 2007. www.nytimes.com.

# SOURCE NOTES CONTINUED

31. Quoted in Thom Shanker, Michael S. Schmidt, and Robert F. Worth, "In Baghdad, Panetta Leads Uneasy Moment of Closure," *New York Times*, December 15, 2011. www.nytimes.com.

32. Quoted in Suadad Al-Salhy and Tim Arango, "Sunni Militants Drive Iraqi Army out of Mosul," *New York Times*, June 10, 2014. www.nytimes.com.

33. Quoted in Al-Salhy and Arango, "Sunni Militants Drive Iraqi Army out of Mosul."

34. "President Obama Makes a Statement on the Crisis in Iraq," *White House*, August 7, 2014. http://obamawhitehouse.archives.gov.

35. "President Obama Makes a Statement on the Crisis in Iraq."

36. "President Obama Makes a Statement on the Crisis in Iraq."

37. Quoted in Liz Sly, "Islamic State May Still Have 30,000 Fighters in Iraq and Syria Even After Setbacks," *Washington Post*, August 14, 2018. www.washingtonpost.com.

## Chapter 3: What Is the Syrian Civil War?

38. Quoted in Rania Abouzeid, "Bouazizi: The Man Who Set Himself and Tunisia on Fire," *Time*, January 21, 2011. www.time.com.

39. Jamie Tarabay, "For Many Syrians, the Story of the War Began with Graffiti in Dara'a," *CNN*, March 15, 2018. www.cnn.com.

40. Quoted in "Syria Prime Minister Riad Hijab Defects," *BBC News*, August 6, 2012. www.bbc.com.

41. Quoted in Ian Black and Martin Chulov, "Syria Crisis: Three of Assad's Top Chiefs Killed in Rebel Bomb Strike," *Guardian*, July 18, 2012. www.theguardian.com.

42. Quoted in Bethan McKernan, "Ghouta Chemical Attack," *Independent*, August 20, 2017. www.independent.co.uk.

43. Quoted in Kareem Shaneen, "Dozens Killed in Suspected Chemical Attack on Syrian Rebel Enclave," *Guardian*, April 8, 2018. www.theguardian.com.

44. Quoted in Petra Cahill, "In Battle Against ISIS in Syria and Iraq, Civilians Suffer Most," *NBC News*, July 8, 2017. www.nbcnews.com.

45. Stuart Jeffries, "ISIS's Destruction of Palmyra: 'The Heart Has Been Ripped Out of the City,'" *Guardian*, September 2, 2015. www.theguardian.com.

46. Quoted in Michael R. Gordon, Helene Cooper, and Michael D. Shear, "Dozens of US Missiles Hit Air Base in Syria," *New York Times*, April 6, 2017. www.nytimes.com.

47. "Statement by Mr. Paulo Sérgio Pinheiro, Chair of the Independent International Commission of Inquiry on the Syrian Arab Republic," *UN Human Rights Office of the High Commissioner*, June 14, 2017. www.ohchr.org.

48. Quoted in "Syria/Russia: International Inaction as Civilians Die," *Human Rights Watch*, February 22, 2018. www.hrw.org.

49. Quoted in "A Look at US Involvement in Syria's Civil War," *Military Times*, December 19, 2018. www.militarytimes.com.

# Chapter 4: Where Else Have Terror and War Happened?

50. Quoted in Shaun Walker, "Ukraine's EU Trade Deal Will Be Catastrophic, Says Russia," *Guardian*, September 22, 2013. www.theguardian.com.

51. "The Situation Room Transcripts: Deal in Ukraine; Crisis in Venezuela," *CNN*, February 21, 2014. http://edition.cnn.com.

52. Quoted in Phil Black, Chelsea J. Carter, and Victoria Butenko, "Ukraine's President Calls Efforts to Push Him from Office a 'Coup,'" *CNN*, February 22, 2014. www.cnn.com.

53. Quoted in Steven Lee Myers and Ellen Barry, "Putin Reclaims Crimea for Russia and Bitterly Denounces the West," *New York Times*, March 18, 2014. www.nytimes.com.

54. Quoted in Dionne Searcey, "Kidnapped as Schoolgirls by Boko Haram: Here They Are Now," *NY Times*, April 11, 2018. www.nytimes.com.

55. Quoted in Dionne Searcey, "Boko Haram Strapped Suicide Bombs to Them. Somehow These Teenage Girls Survived," *New York Times*, October 25, 2017. www.nytimes.com.

56. Quoted in Ahmed Al-Haj, "Saudis' Operation Decisive Storm in Yemen a 'Dangerous Step,' Iran Warns," *Globe and Mail*, March 26, 2015. www.theglobeandmail.com.

57. Quoted in Charlene Gubash, "Yemen, Africa Crisis Is Largest in the World, Aid Agencies Say," *NBC News*, July 30, 2017. www.nbcnews.com.

58. Quoted in Yuliya Talmazan, "Yemen Crisis: Three Stats That Reveal the Scale of World's Worst Humanitarian Crisis," *NBC News*, October 28, 2018. www.nbcnews.com.

59. Quoted in Dominic Dudley, "Where and Why the World Is Getting More Dangerous," *Forbes*, June 6, 2018. www.forbes.com.

# FOR FURTHER RESEARCH

## Books

John Allen, *Thinking Critically: Terrorism*. San Diego, CA: ReferencePoint Press, 2018.

Michael Capek, *The Syrian Conflict*. Minneapolis, MN: Abdo Publishing, 2017.

Robert Green, *Debates on the 9/11 Attacks*. San Diego, CA: ReferencePoint Press, 2018.

Hal Marcowitz, *The War on ISIS*. San Diego, CA: ReferencePoint Press, 2018.

Don Nardo, *Cause & Effect: The War on Terror*. San Diego, CA: ReferencePoint Press, 2018.

## Internet Sources

"From the Editors: The Times and Iraq," *New York Times*, May 26, 2004. www.nytimes.com.

Laura Kasinof, "How the Houthis Did It," *Foreign Policy*, January 23, 2015. www.foreignpolicy.com.

"Kidnapped as Schoolgirls by Boko Haram," *New York Times*, April 11, 2018. www.nytimes.com.

Nicholas Schmidle, "Getting bin Laden," *New Yorker*, August 8, 2011. www.newyorker.com.

# Websites

### Amnesty International
**www.amnesty.org/en/**

Amnesty International's purpose is to fight abuses of human rights around the world and to aid refugees, migrants, and others who are suffering from the effects of war and terror. The organization accomplishes these goals through research, advocacy, and campaigns of action.

### Human Rights Watch
**www.hrw.org**

Human Rights Watch unites lawyers, journalists, and advocates to help protect the basic human rights of citizens regardless of nationality. The group uses its research, compiled into reports, to push for policy change that will protect human rights for all.

### Oxford Islamic Studies
**www.oxfordislamicstudies.com**

The Oxford Islamic Studies website is an online resource for those wishing to learn more about Islam, with contributions by leading scholars in the field. The site is dedicated to growing and promoting understanding of the Islamic faith and the Islamic world.

### United Nations
**www.un.org/en/**

The United Nations, founded in 1945 to help prevent future world wars, seeks to maintain international peace and security. The organization strives to end or prevent conflict through mediation and peacekeeping forces.

# INDEX

# INDEX CONTINUED

# IMAGE CREDITS

# ABOUT THE AUTHOR

Blythe Lawrence is a journalist from Seattle.